THE FRANK GAMBALE TECHNIQUE BOOK II

by FRANK GAMBALE

CREDITS

Music Editor........................Wayne King

Music Copy........................Frank Gambale, Iain Scott

Typesetting........................Jon Morgan

Special thanks to Jon Morgan for countless hours of dedication to both tech books and to Craig Garfinkle for introducing Frank to Mark back in '85.

Stream or download the audio content for this book.
To access, visit: **alfred.com/redeem**
Enter the following code: 00-MMBK0003CD_225522

SOLOING CONCEPT

I break music down into six basic chord types, and their applicable scales (See Fig. 1). Then over each of the chord types I apply five soloing approaches for each applicable scale. The possibilities for soloing over these chords are, therefore, greatly expanded.

This book covers the second and third approaches for chord type 4 and all approaches for chord types 5 and 6.

CHORD TYPES
(and applicable scales)

1   MINOR 7
   1a Dorian
   1b Aeolian

2   MAJOR 7
   2a Major
   2b Lydian

3   UNALTERED DOMINANT 7
   3a Mixolydian
   3b Lydian b7

4   ALTERED DOMINANT 7
   4a Super Locrian
   4b Diminished 1/2 / whole
   4c Phrygian major

5   MINOR 7 (b5)
   5a Locrian
   5b Aeolian b5
   5c Locrian nat6

6   DIMINISHED
   6a Diminished whole / 1/2
   6b Super Locrian nat6

APPROACHES

1   SCALE*
   (7 or 8 notes)

2   PENTATONICS & BLUES
   (5 & 6 notes)

3   ARPEGGIOS
   (4 notes)

4   TRIADS
   (3 notes)

5   INTERVALS
   (2 notes)

---

*   Approaches 2 through 5 are derived from the applicable scale chosen for soloing approach 1.

Fig. 1

Audio Tracking Information

1 Song & Introduction
2 Diminished ½ Whole Scale Examples 1–2
3 Example 3
4 Example 4
5 Example 5
6 E Phrygian Examples 1–2
7 Arpeggios Example 3
8 Triads Examples 4–5
9 Lowanna Street
10 Locrian Examples 1–2
11 Arpeggios Example 3
12 Triads & Intervals Examples 4–5
13 Aeolian Examples 1–2
14 Arpeggios & Triads Examples 3–5
15 Scales & Arps Examples 1–3
16 Triads & Intervals Examples 4–5
17 Beef Intolorable
18 Diminished Examples 1–2
19 Arpeggios Example 3
20 Triads & Intervals Examples 4–5
21 Mode VII Harmonic Minor Examples 1–3
22 Arpeggios Example 3
23 Triads Examples 4–5
24 Cleo & Rebecca

Chapter 4

Continued from Book One

ALTERED DOMINANTS

DIMINISHED 1/2 WHOLE SCALE

Now, I would like to mention some other scales and chords that don't fit the SUPER LOCRIAN (7th mode MELODIC MINOR) scale.

There are two different scale choices depending on the character of the altered chord. These are:

1. The DIMINISHED 1/2 WHOLE SCALE.

2. MODE 5 OF THE HARMONIC MINOR SCALE.
   In this chapter we'll look at the Diminished 1/2 whole scale.

The diminished scale is sometimes referred to as the symmetrical scale because its construction is always 1/2 steps and whole steps. (whole, 1/2 whole, 1/2) or (1/2, whole, 1/2 whole etc.). The diminished scale beginning with a whole step is the scale used for straight diminished chords e. g. C dim. = C diminished scale (whole, 1/2 whole, 1/2 . . . C D Eb F Gb Ab A B C).

For Altered Dominant chords we play the inversion of this scale, and compare it to a C major scale.

```
C MAJOR     =  C   D   E   F   G  A  B   =    1   2   3    4    5    6    7
C DIM. DOM. =  C Db  Eb E    F# G  A  Bb  =    1  b2  b3 3      b5 5     6 b7
```

Diagram #1
E Dim 1/2 Whole

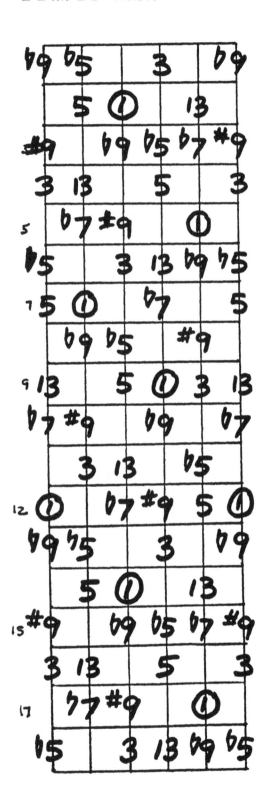

Within this octave we see several possibilities for chords. We can easily see the Dominant 7 (1 3 5 b7). If we use 1 3 5 b7, we are left with b2, b3 and b5 and 6. The b2 and b3 are the same as b9 and #9 e.g. in the key of C, the b2 and b3 are the notes Db and D#. Db is also the b9 of C and D# is also the #9 of C. In the key of C, the b5 = F# which is the same as #11 and the 6 = A which is the same as 13 in the 2nd octave.

So the scale intervals for two octaves are as follows:

1 (b2 b3) 3 (b5) 5 (6) b7   b9   #9   #11   13.

The DIMINISHED 1/2 WHOLE scale differs from the SUPER LOCRIAN (Melodic Minor 7th mode) by two notes. Knowing which they are and what they sound like in a dominant 7 chord, will help you determine which scale to choose. The two notes are the Natural 5 and 13 (6).

So, an altered dominant chord, e. g. C7b9 with a 13, definitely belongs to the diminished 1/2 whole scale. The 13, or 6, is the note in an altered chord that confirms this scale choice. The natural 5 is more ambiguous because it is also part of the 5th mode of Harmonic minor (next chapter) .

So for all our examples of a Diminished Dominant chord, we'll use a 13b9. Other options could be 13b9# 11, 13#9, or simply, C7b9 or C7. I will specify the chord for the examples.

EXAMPLE 1. E DIMINISHED 1/2 WHOLE over E13b9

PENTATONIC SCALES AND THE DIMINISHED DOMINANT SCALE

Pentatonics within this scale... well, there are no standard major or minor pentatonics within this scale. But that never stopped me, and it, as you will soon discover, won't stop you either. At this point, we have to transgress the rules, which for me, was one of the best ways to discover new things (as long as you don't hurt anybody !) .

Let's make up some pentatonic scales. Here are some of the possibilities:

1.   1 b3 b5 5 b7
2.   1 b3 3 5 b7
3.   1 b3 b5 6 b7
4.   1 b2 3 5 b7
5.   1 b2 b3 5 b7
6.   1 b2 b3 b5 6
7.   1 b2 3 b5 b7   etc., etc., etc. . . . .

There are lots of different 5 note scales (pentatonics), as you can see. None of these, however, conform to any standard pentatonic. But nevertheless, some of these hybrids sound very interesting indeed. For the examples here I've chosen numbers 1 and 4.

EXAMPLE 2 (a)   HYBRID PENTATONIC NO. 1   1 b3 b5 5 b7 over E13b9

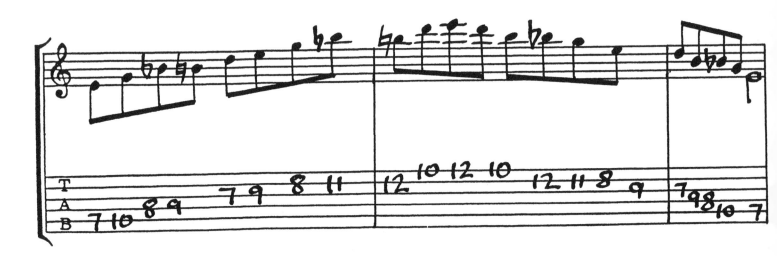

4

EXAMPLE 2 (b)   *HYBRID PENTATONIC NO. 4*   *1 b2 3 5 b7 over El3b9*

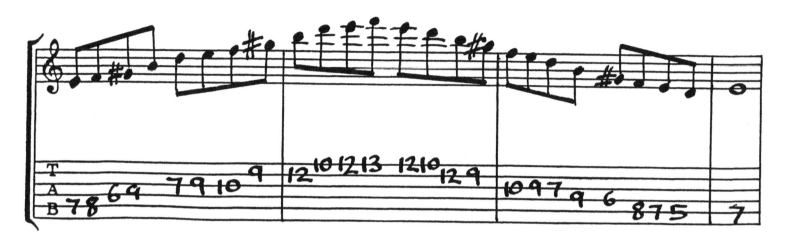

* Note: EVERYTHING IN THIS SCALE CAN BE SHIFTED AND PLAYED IN MINOR 3rd INTERVALS. IN OTHER WORDS, IF YOU HAVE AN "E" HYBRID PENTATONIC SCALE, TRY PLAYING THE SAME SHAPE SYMMETRICALLY, STARTING ON "G" THEN "Bb" AND "C#". DON'T FORGET THAT THIS SCALE IS SYMMETRICAL.

ANOTHER TIP IS TO PLAY SEQUENCES IN INTERVALS OF b5'S (TRITONE) , eg. "E" HYBRID PENTATONIC FOLLOWED BY A "Bb" HYBRID PENTATONIC. THE REASON THIS WORKS IS THAT 2 MINOR 3RD INTERVALS EQUAL ONE TRITONE.

ARPEGGIOS IN THE 1/2 WHOLE DIMINISHED SCALE.

1 b2 b3 3 b5 5 6 b7

Once again we see that there are many possible four note chord arpeggios available from this scale. Let's look at some of them.

1.	1 b3 b5 b7	= min 7b5
2.	1 3 5 b7	= dom7
3.	1 b3 5 b7	= min7
4.	1 3 b5 b7	= dom7b5
5.	1 3 5 6	= maj6
6.	1 b3 5 6	= min6

All these arpeggios can be played over El3b9, starting on either E, G, Bb, or C# (thanks to the powers of symmetry.) .

5

EXAMPLE 3.   ARPEGGIOS 1-6 OVER El3b9

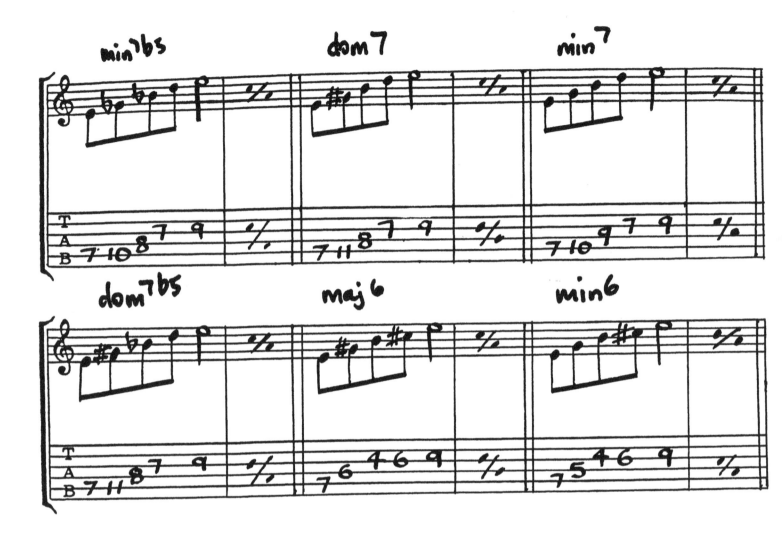

TRIADS IN THE 1/2 WHOLE DIMINISHED SCALE

There are three triads available to us in this scale.

1. 1 3 5   = maj
2. 1 b3 5   = min
3. 1 b3 b5   = dim

This gives Emaj, Emin, and Edim triads to listen to over El3b9. Don't forget, these triads can also begin with a G, Bb, or C#.

6

EXAMPLE 4 (a -c) E MAJOR TRIAD OVER E13b9
E MINOR TRIAD OVER E13b9
E DIM. TRIAD OVER E13b9

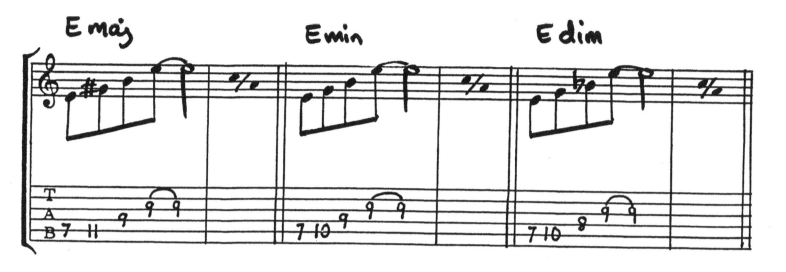

EXAMPLE 4 (d)   E, G, Bb, AND C# MAJOR TRIADS OVER E13b9

EXAMPLE 4 (e)   *E, G, Bb, AND C# MINOR TRIADS OVER E13b9*

EXAMPLE 4 (f)   *E, G, Bb, AND C# DIM. TRIADS OVER E13b9*

8

INTERVALS IN 1/2 WHOLE DIMINISHED

Min 3rd, 3rd, b5, 5th, 6th are all available to us from the root of the scale and they can also be played symmetrically in minor 3rds and b5ths, etc.

Other intervals, such as 4ths and b6ths, are also available, however, not beginning on the root of the scale. These intervals appear a 1/2 step above the root and then symmetrically in minor 3rds and b5ths from there.

Minor 3rds, b5ths, and 6ths can be played parallel up and down the scale.

EXAMPLE 5 (a)   MINOR 3RDS PARALLEL OVER E13b9

EXAMPLE 5 (b)   b5THS PARALLEL OVER E13b9

9

EXAMPLE 5 (c)   *6THS PARALLEL OVER E13b9*

EXAMPLE 5 (d)   *4THS IN MINOR 3RDS OVER E13b9*

EXAMPLE 5 (e)   *6THS IN b5THS OVER E13b9*

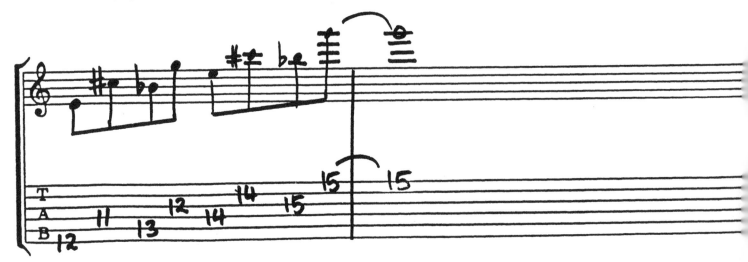

HARMONIC MINOR OVER ALTERED DOMINANT CHORDS

Dominant chords fall on the 5th degree of the Harmonic Minor scale. So, if we have an E7b9, A Harmonic Minor scale can be used. The notes of an A Harmonic Minor scale are:

A B C D E F G# = 1 2 b3 4 5 b6 7

It is very important to learn the mode from the root of the chord; and so we need to learn the interval structure of the 5th mode of Harmonic Minor.

A B C D E F G# beginning on E = E F G# A B C D

So to find out the interval structure of this 5th mode, we must use our trusty old standard, the major scale , and compare notes.

E MAJOR = E F# G# A B C# D# = 1 2 3 4 5 6 7

5TH MODE A HARM MIN = E F G# A B C D = 1 b2 3 4 5 b6 b7

* This mode will be referred to from now on as the PHRYGIAN MAJOR SCALE.

The second octave of this mode reveals the upper extensions.

E F G# A B C D E F G# A B C = 1 b2 3 4 5 b6 b7 8 b9 10 11 b13

Now we can see the types of chords available. 1, 3, 5, b7 gives us our dominant 7 character, which leaves us with a b2, 4, and b6. b2 = b9. 4 = 11. b6 = #5 = b13.

E Phrygian Major Over E7b9

E Phrygian Major

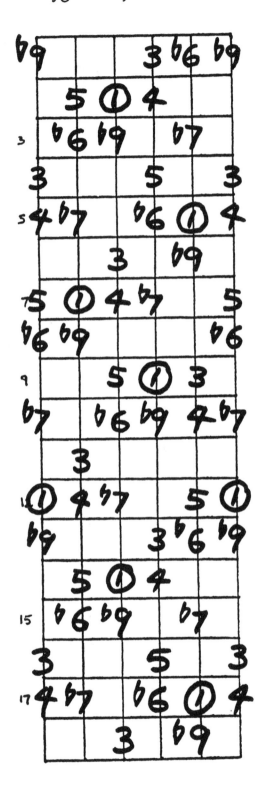

So now we need to figure which dominant chord is specifically a Phrygian Major chord.

Well, in the last approach we discovered that the diminished dominant chord with a natural 13 (6) was specifically diminished 1/2 whole scale.

The combination of 1, 3, 5, b7 with a #5 is specifically Phrygian Major. In other words, the natural 5 and #5 only occur together with this scale.

Note also the absence of the #9. E7#9 would be either Super Locrian or Diminished 1/2 Whole.

Now this is all well and good in theory and on paper, but it is rare to hear the 5 and the #5 together in a voicing of a dominant chord; what IS important is that you become familiar with the chords of the harmonized Harmonic Minor scale so you will recognize a Harmonic Minor chord progression, e. g.

Dmin7 E7b9 Amin or Fmaj7 E7b9 Amin

Another great way to determine which scale is intended, and this is overlooked by a lot of musicians, is to study the melody of the tune to discover what the composer intended. This, in my experience, is the best approach, especially when the chords written are vague, like e. g. E7 to Amin.

So for my music examples I have chosen an E7b9 chord.

At this point, I'd like to give you examples of each of the three possibilities of altered dominant chords at work.

EXAMPLE 1. SUPER LOCRIAN (MELODIC MINOR UP 1/2 STEP)
In this example, the melody begins #9, 3, b7, #5, 3, #9, B9, B7, #9. You will notice that the only scale which incorporates the #5 and b5 and #9 and b9, is the Super Locrian.

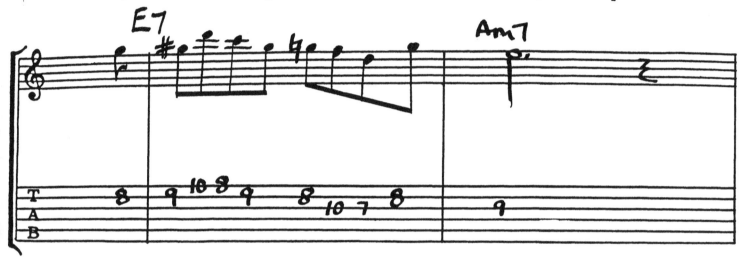

EXAMPLE 2. DIMINISHED 1/2 WHOLE (DIMINISHED DOMINANT)
In this example, the melody is a 13, Root, 13, 3, 5. This has to be Diminished 1/2 Whole because of the 13th and natural 5.

EXAMPLE 3. *PHRYGIAN MAJOR (MODE V HARMONIC MINOR)*

In this example the melody has the 5, #5, 5, 3, b9, #5. This has to be Phrygian Major because it is the only altered scale which includes the #5 and natural 5.

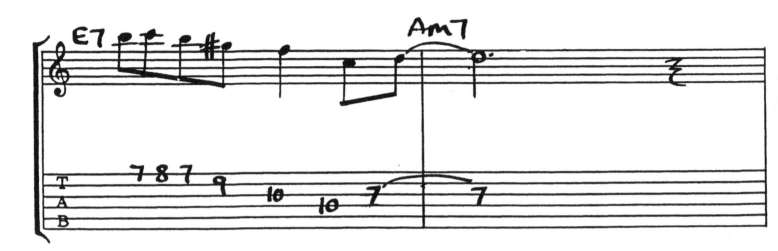

Now let's take a look at the harmonized scale chords found in the Harmonic Minor scale.

A HARMONIC MINOR = A B C D E F G#

CHORD 1 = A C E G# = Amin (maj7)
CHORD 2 = B D F A   = Bmin7b5
CHORD 3 = C E G# B = Cmaj7#5
CHORD 4 = D F A C   = Dmin7
CHORD 5 = E G# B D = E7
CHORD 6 = F A C E   = Fmaj7
CHORD 7 = G# B D F = G#dim7

Amin (maj7), Bmin7, Cmaj7#5, Dmin7, E7, Fmaj7, G#dim7

PENTATONICS IN PHRYGIAN MAJOR

Once again we have a situation where there are no standard pentatonic scales. So once again, let's make up some of our own. To do this, we must look at the interval structure of the Phrygian Major scale.

Phrygian Major = E F G# A B C D = 1 b2 3 4 5 b6 b7

EXAMPLE 2 (a)   -   HYBRID 1 = 1 b2 3 5 b7   over E7b9

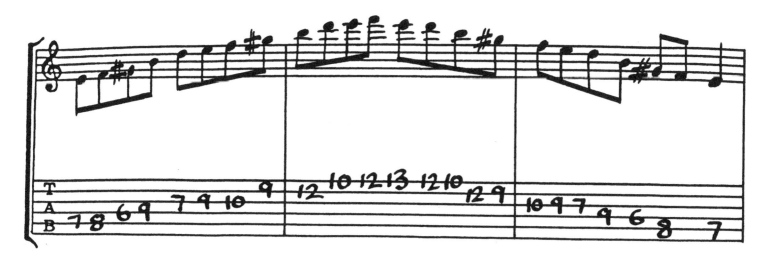

EXAMPLE 2 (b)   -   HYBRID 2 = 1 b2 4 5 b7   over E7b9

EXAMPLE 2 (c)   -   HYBRID 3 = 1 3 4 5 b7   over E7b9

ARPEGGIO'S IN THE PHRYGIAN MAJOR

Now we'll listen to all the diatonic arpeggios from the Phrygian Major scale, and hear how they sound over an E7b9 chord. Using E as our root of the Phrygian Major scale, we'll listen to:

E7 Fmaj7 G#dim7 Amin7 Bmin7b5 Cmaj7#5 Dmin7.

EXAMPLE 3 (a)   *E7 arp over E7b9*

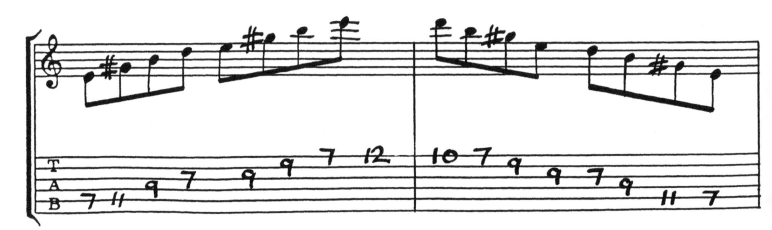

EXAMPLE 3 (b)   *Fmaj7 over E7b9*

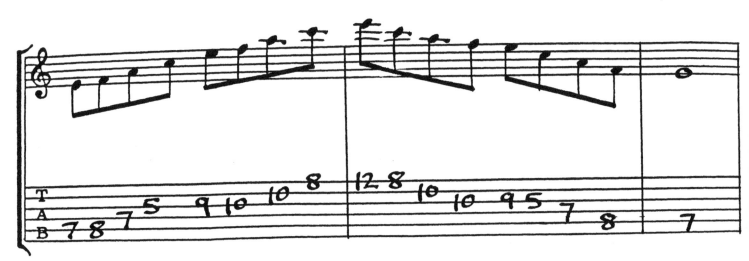

16

EXAMPLE 3 (c)   G#dim7 over E7b9

EXAMPLE 3 (d)   Amin (maj7) over E7b9

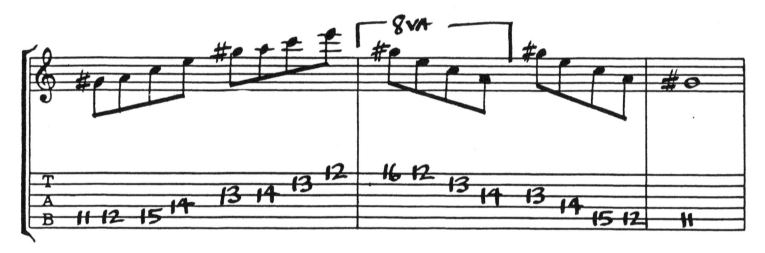

EXAMPLE 3 (e)   Bmin7b5 over E7b9

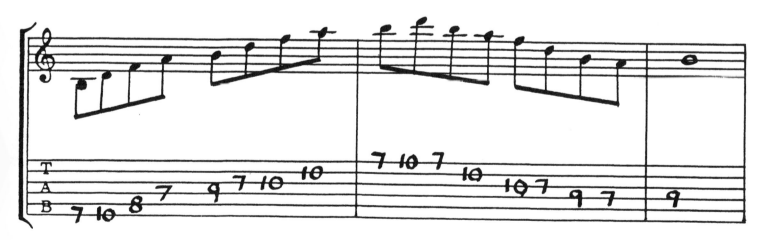

EXAMPLE 3 (f)   Cmaj#5 over E7b9

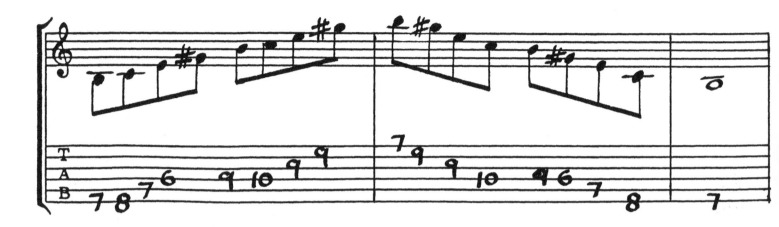

EXAMPLE 3 (g)   Dmin7 over E7b9

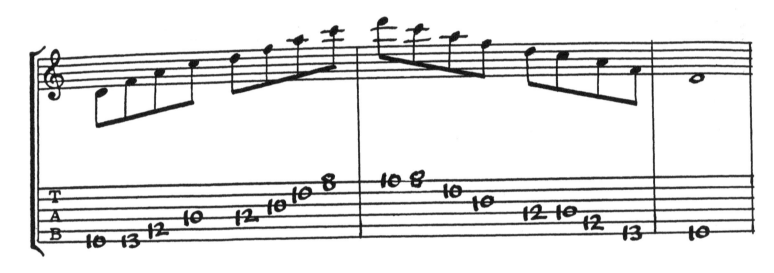

TRIADS FROM THE PHRYGIAN MAJOR

In the A Harmonic minor scale there are two major triads. They are on the 5th and 6th degrees. E major and F major triads. Let's take a listen to each of these.

EXAMPLE 4 (a)   *E MAJOR TRIAD OVER E7b7*

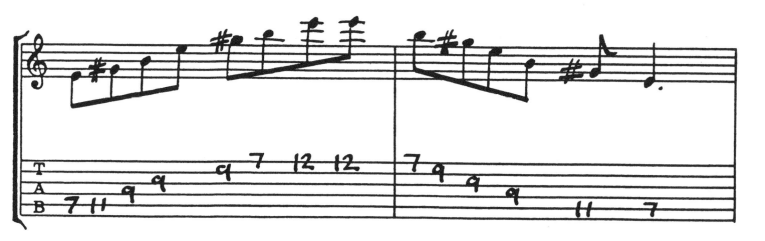

EXAMPLE 4 (b)   *F MAJOR TRIAD OVER E7b9*

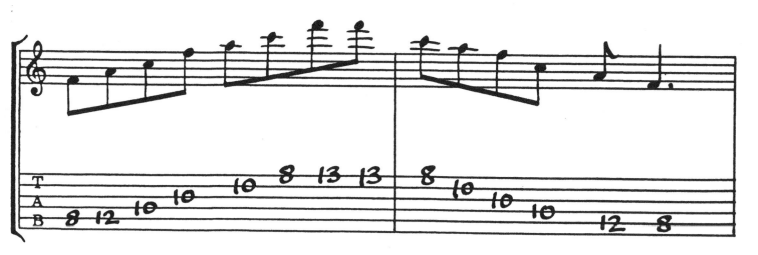

DON'T FORGET THAT ALL THE DIATONIC TRIADS WORK WELL; ie., Amin, Bdim, Caug, Dmin, E, F, G#dim.

EXAMPLE 4 (c) ALL DIATONIC TRIADS FROM E PHRYGIAN MAJOR

INTERVALS IN THE PHRYGIAN MAJOR

I have found that 3rds and 6ths work the best in this inconsistent scale. Let's listen.

EXAMPLE 5 (a) DIATONIC 3RDS IN PHRYGIAN MAJOR OVER E7b9

EXAMPLE 5 (b) DIATONIC 6THS IN PHRYGIAN MAJOR OVER E7b9

END OF CHAPTER SUMMARY

Now let's look back at all the altered chord scales and I will point out the approaches that I have found most useful.

CHORD = E7#5b9   **FORMULA**

SCALE CHOICE = E Super Locrian   =   1 b2 b3 3 b5 #5 b7
same as F Melodic Minor - up a 1/2 step.   b9 #9   #11 b13

PENTATONIC/BLUES = G Minor Pentatonic or Blues - up a min 3rd

ARPEGGIO = Dmin7b5 or G#maj7#5 - down whole step min7b5 and up a 3rd maj7#5 (This could also be visualized as down a 1/2 step from the 1 chord in a 5 to 1 chord progression; e. g., E7b9 to Amin7, the G#maj7#5 arpeggio on the E7b9 chord has a root a 1/2 step from the root of the chord to which it is leading.).

TRIADS = Bb and C major - triads from the b5 and #5 of the chord.

INTERVALS = 3rds or 6ths (they are inversions of one another).

CHORD = E13b9   **FORMULA**

SCALE = Diminished 1/2 whole   1 b2 b3 3 b5 6 b7
        from E G Bb or C# roots.   b9 #9 #11 13

PENTATONIC = Hybrid   1 b2 3 5 b7 from E G Bb or C# Roots

ARPEGGIOS = major 6 arps   from E G Bb or C# roots.

TRIADS = C# major   from the 6th degree of the chord.

INTERVALS = Minor 3rds.

CHORD = E7b9   **FORMULA**

SCALE = E Phrygian Major   1 b2 3 4 5 b6 b7 b9 11 b13
      Mode 5 of A Harmonic minor.

PENTATONIC = Hybrid   1 3 4 5 b7.

ARPEGGIO = C Major7#5   Major7#5 from the #5 of E.

TRIADS = E and F major   Root and up a 1/2 step.

INTERVALS = 3rds.

21

PROGRESSIONS USING ALTERED DOMINANTS

PROGRESSION 1.　　　　A Dorian to E Super Locrian.

II:　　Amin7　　　I　　%　　I　　E7#5#9　　I　　%　　:II

PROGRESSION 2.　　　　E Dorian to B 1/2 Whole Diminished.

II:　　Emin7　　　I　　%　　I　　B13b9　　I　　%　　:II

PROGRESSION 3.　　　　C Dorian to D Phrygian Major.

II:　　Cmin7　　　I　　%　　I　　D7b9　　　I　　%　　:II

COMBINATION PROGRESSIONS

PROGRESSION 1.　"NORTHBOURNE AVENUE"

　　　A Dorian - D Lydianb7 - F Lydian - E Super Locrian.

II:　　Amin7　　　I　　%　　I　　D9　　I　　%　　I

I　　Fmaj7　　　I　　%　　I　E7#5b9　I　　%　　:II

PROGRESSION 2.　　　　E Dorian - A 1/2 Whole Dim. - D major - B Super Locrian.

II:　　Emin7　　　I　　%　　I A13b9　I　　%　　I

I　　Dmaj7　　　I　　%　　I B7#5b9　I　　%　　:II

PROGRESSION 3.　　　　C Aeolian - G Phrygian Major or G Super Locrian - C Dorian

- F Mixolydian - F 1/2 Whole Dim. - Bb Major - Eb Super Locrian

- Ab Major - G Mixolydian - G Phrygian Major or G Super Locrian.

II:　　Cmin7　　　I　　%　　I　　G7b9　　I　　%　　I

I　　Cmin7　　　I　　%　　I　　Eb/F　　I　　F7b9　　I

I　　Bbmaj7　　I　　%　　I　Eb7#5#9　I　　%　　I

I　　Abmaj7　　I　　%　　I　　F/G　　I　　G7b9　　:II

"Lowanna Street"
(Based On Progression #3)

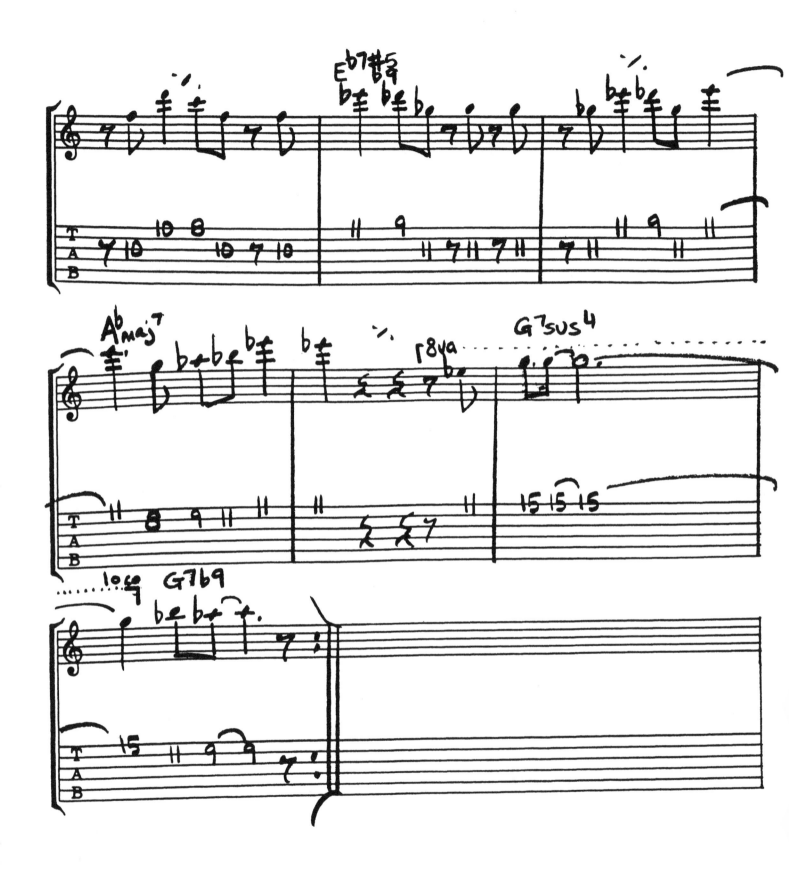

CHAPTER 5

THE MINOR 7b5 CHORD

D LOCRIAN

There are three main ways to treat the minor 7b5 chord. It could be the VII chord of the Major scale, or chord VI of the Melodic Minor scale, or chord II of the Harmonic Minor scale.

During this chapter we'll discuss the differences between them.

The first type we'll discuss is the min7b5 as a VII chord Major, and our chord will be Dmin7b5.

Dmin7b5 = chord VII of Eb Major = D LOCRIAN.

LOCRIAN INTERVAL STRUCTURE FROM D compared to D major.

```
D Eb F G Ab Bb C  =  1 b2 b3 4 b5 b6 b7.
                       b9 #9 11 #11 b13
D E F# G A B C#   =  1 2 3 4 5 6 7
                       9 11 13
```

Eb Harmonized Major

Ebmaj7   Fmin7   Gmin7   Abmaj7   Bb7   Cmin7   Dmin7b5

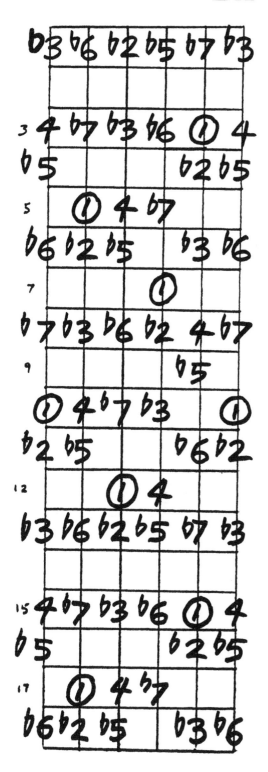

25

EXAMPLE 1.
D Locrian Over Dmin7b5

PENTATONICS FROM D LOCRIAN OVER D MIN7b5

Remember from our previous discovery that there are three minor pentatonics in any major scale located on the II, III, and VI degrees. Well we know that D Locrian is the same as Eb Major, then theoretically, the II, III, and VI of Eb will provide us with the roots of the three minor pentatonics. They are as follows:

Over Dmin7b5 we can play F, G, or C Minor Pentatonics.

EXAMPLE 2 (a)   *F Min Pentatonic over Dmin7b5.*

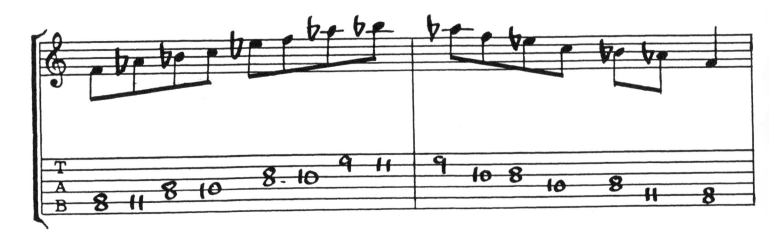

EXAMPLE 2 (b)   *G Min Pentatonic over Dmin7b5.*

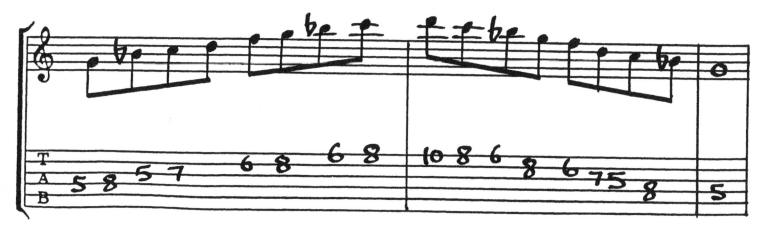

EXAMPLE 2 (c)   *C Min Pentatonic over Dmin7b5.*

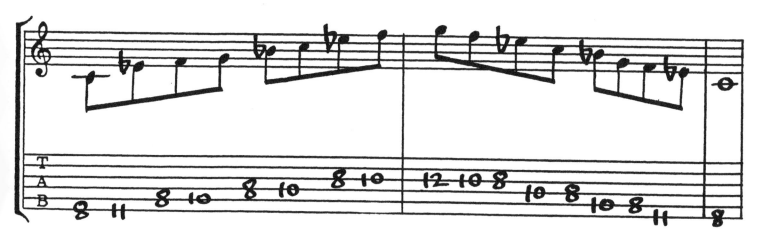

ARPEGGIOS FROM D LOCRIAN OVER DMIN7b5

The arpeggio possibilities for D Locrian will be derived from the Eb Major scale. Once again, the Harmonized scale.

Ebmaj7   Fmin7   Gmin7   Abmaj7   Bb7   Cmin7   Dmin7b5

Now we're going to listen to all of the seven diatonic arpeggios over Dmin7b5. Remember that not all these arps sound good, but this is the approach we must take to find the ones that do sound good; and when you find one that sounds good, believe me, it's obvious, so bear with me.

NOTE There is a trick to making the not so good sounding arpeggios sound better, and that is by beginning and ending these arps with a chord tone. All the arpeggios will have at least one tone directly related to the chord, so start and end on that tone.

Let's say you wanted to play a Gmin7 arp on the Dmin7b5. Dmin7b5 = D F Ab C. The Gmin7 = G Bb D F. Begin and end the Gmin7 arp with one of the two available common chord tones, in this case either D or F.

EXAMPLE 3 (a)   *Ebmaj7 arpeggio over Dmin7b5*

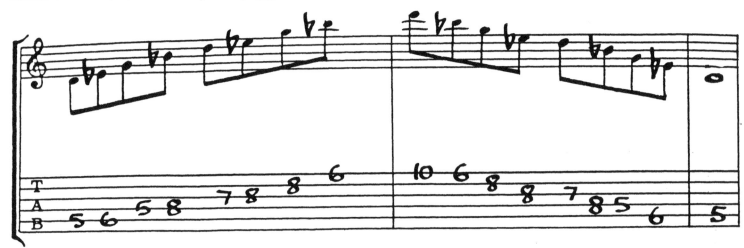

EXAMPLE 3 (b)   *Fmin7 arpeggio over Dmin7b5*

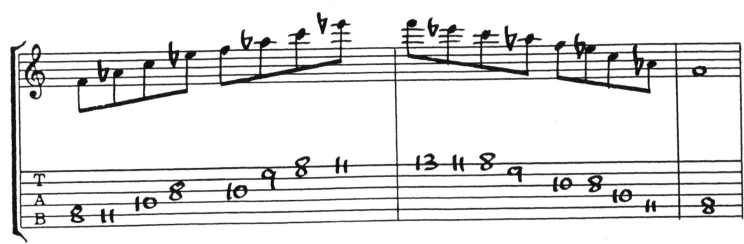

EXAMPLE 3 (c)   Gmin7 arpeggio over Dmin7b5

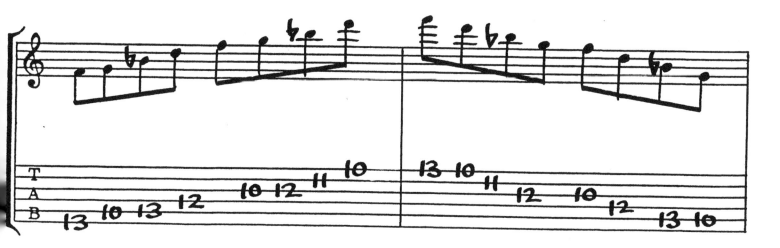

EXAMPLE 3 (d)   Abmaj7 arpeggio over Dmin7b5

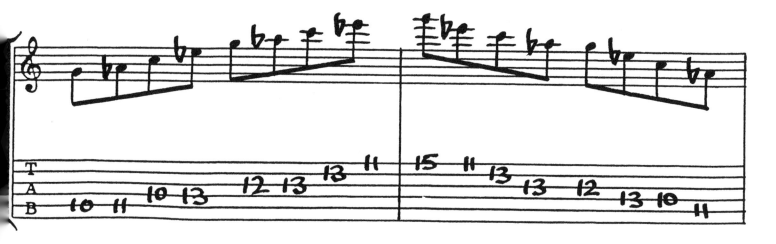

EXAMPLE 3 (e)   Bb7 arpeggio over Dmin7b5

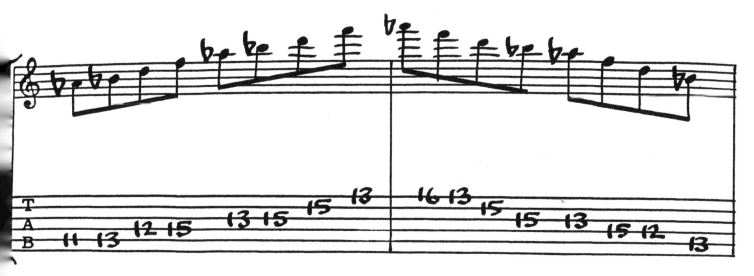

EXAMPLE 3 (f)   *Cmin7 arpeggio over Dmin7b5*

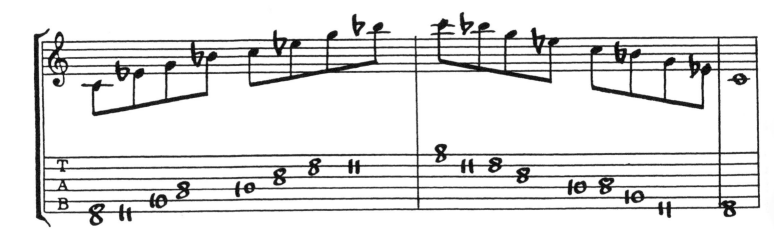

EXAMPLE 3 (g)   *Dmin7b5 arpeggio over Dmin7b5.*

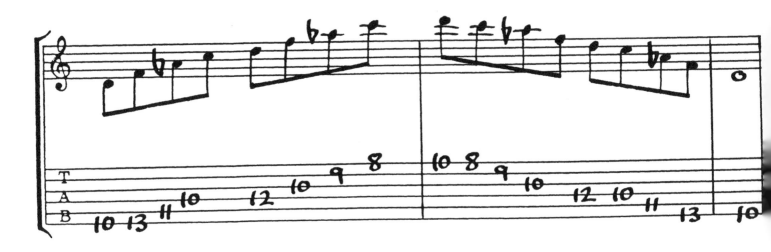

30

TRIADS IN D LOCRIAN OVER D MIN7b5

Let's take the three major triads from Eb Major and listen to them over Dmin7b5. They are as follows:

I IV V triads from Eb = Eb Ab and Bb.

EXAMPLE 4 (a)   *Eb Major triad over Dmin7b5*

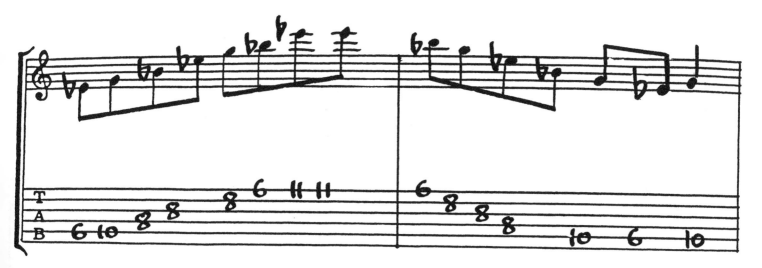

EXAMPLE 4 (b)   *Ab Major triad over Dmin7b5*

31

EXAMPLE 4 (c)   *Bb Major triad over Dmin7b5*

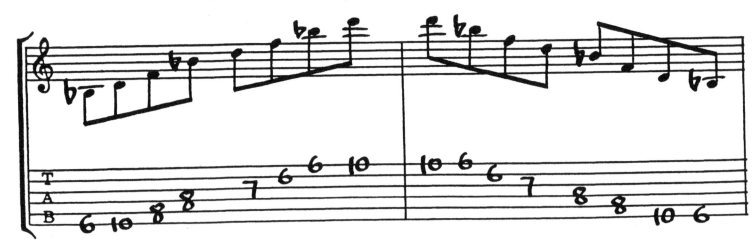

    * Don't forget that all the diatonic triads from Eb Major are worth listening to.

EXAMPLE 4 (d)   *All diatonic triads from Eb Major over Dmin7b5: Ebmaj, Fmin, Gmin, Abmaj, Bbmaj, Cmin, Ddim.*

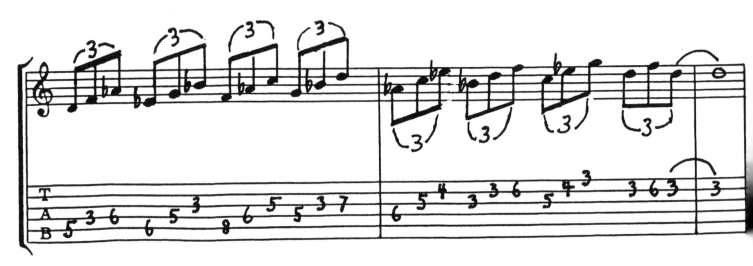

INTERVALS IN D LOCRIAN OVER D MINb5.

Let's take a listen to diatonic 3rds, 4ths, 5ths, and 6ths.

EXAMPLE 5 (a)   *Diatonic 3rds in D Locrian over Dmin7b5.*

EXAMPLE 5 (b)   *Diatonic 4ths in D Locrian over Dmin7b5.*

EXAMPLE 5 (c)   *Diatonic 5ths in D Locrian over Dmin7b5.*

EXAMPLE 5 (d)   *Diatonic 6ths in D Locrian over Dmin7b5.*

SUMMARY OF CHAPTER 5. DMIN7b5 AS CHORD VII MAJOR.

CHORD = D MIN7b5

SCALE = D Locrian

PENTATONIC/BLUES = G Min Pent/Blues.

ARPEGGIOS = Dmin7b5

TRIADS = Ab and Bb

INTERVALS = 4ths

FORMULAS

1 b2 b3 4 b5 b6 b7 b9
#9 11 #11 b13

Up a 4th from root.

arp from root

triads from b5 and #5

34

D MIN7b5 AS VI CHORD MELODIC MINOR

If we treat the minor7b5 chord as the 6th mode of the melodic minor, then we'll be using the Aeolian b5 scale.

The interval structure of D Aeolian b5 compared to a D major scale will be as follows:

Dmin7b5 = chord VI of F Melodic Minor

F Melodic Minor = F G Ab Bb C D E

D Major = D E F# G A B C# D = 1 2 3 4 5 6 7

D Aeolian b5 = D E F G Ab Bb C = 1 2 b3 4 b5 b6 b7
                                              9 #9 11 #11 b13

EXAMPLE 1.
D Aeolian b5 Over Dmin7b5

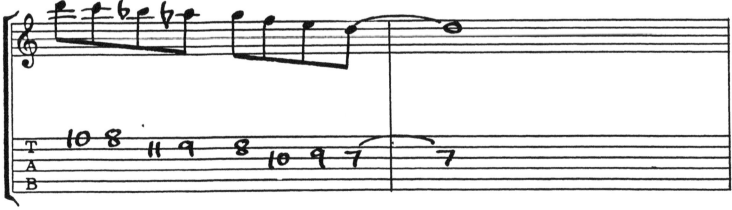

35

D Aeolian b5

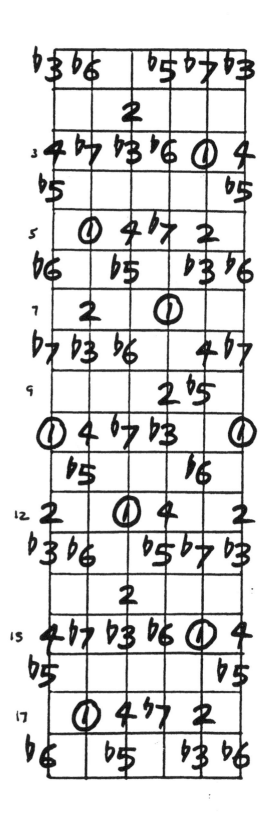

NOTE Notice that the only difference between the Aeolian b5 approach and the Locrian approach is one note. Let's compare:

D Aeolian b5   = D E F G Ab Bb C

D Locrian   =   D Eb F G Ab Bb C

The only difference is the natural 2nd (9th) in the Aeolian b5 or the b2nd (b9) in the Locrian. This might not seem like much of a difference theoretically; however, once you get used to it the natural 9 is a very pleasing and unusual note over the Minor7b5 chord.

PENTATONICS FROM THE D AEOLIAN b5 SCALE OVER Dmin7b5

There is only one Minor pentatonic in the Melodic Minor scale. It occurs on the 2nd degree.

Dmin7b5   =   F melodic minor

2nd degree of F melodic minor is G

So we find that G min Pentatonic is available to us from the D Aeolian b5 scale. However, you'll notice that it is the same Pentatonic that was available to us in the Locrian chapter. So the only route for us is the hybrid pentatonic once again. The first that springs to my mind is a variation of the G min pentatonic; one that will include the only note that changed in this Aeolian b5 approach, namely, an E natural, which is the natural 2 (9) in D.

G MIN PENT. = G Bb C D F

Let's drop the D and make it an E.

We're left with G Bb C E F. Let's name this Hybrid Pentatonic 1.

36

EXAMPLE 2 (a)   *HYBRID PENTATONIC 1 over Dmin7b5*

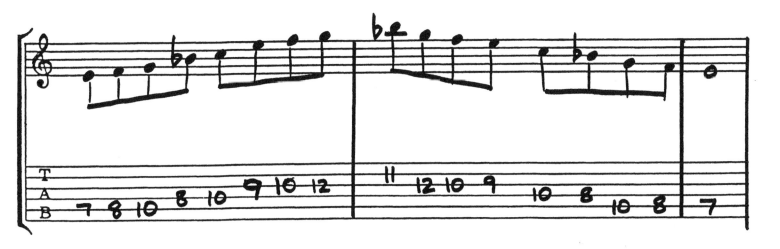

How about using the four notes of the Dmin7b5 chord and adding the natural 2nd (9). We'd have:

D E F Ab C =   1 2 b3 b5 b7

Let's name this Hybrid Pentatonic 2.

EXAMPLE 2 (b)   *HYBRID PENTATONIC 2 over Dmin7b5*

ARPEGGIO'S FROM D AEOLIAN b5 over Dmin7b5

To find the possible arpeggios to play over Dmin7b5 as a VI chord of F Melodic Minor, we must look at the harmonized scale.

Fmin (maj7)   Gmin7   Abmaj7#5   Bb7   C7   Dmin7b5   Emin7b5

All these arps sound good over Dmin7b5. With that in mind, let's zero in on some of the ones that really outline the Aeolian b5 (melodic minor) scale sound. To do this we must use arps that include the natural 2 (9).

Dmin7b5 = 1 b3 b5 b7 = D F Ab C

Let's drop the root and extend the chord to 9.

b3 b5 b7 9 = F Ab C E = Fmin (maj7)

EXAMPLE 3 (a)   Fmin (maj7) Arpeggio over Dmin7b5

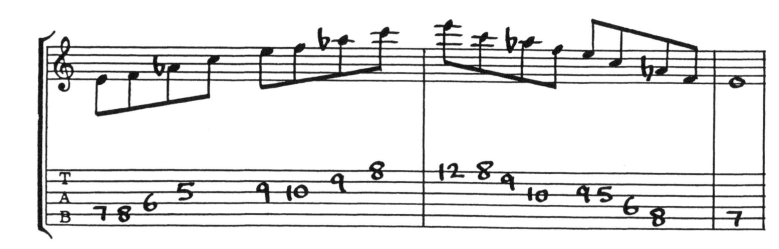

O. K., that worked great. Let's extend the chord further.

b5 b7 9 11 = Ab C E G = Abmaj7#5

38

EXAMPLE 3 (b)   *Abmaj7#5 Arpeggio over Dmin7b5*

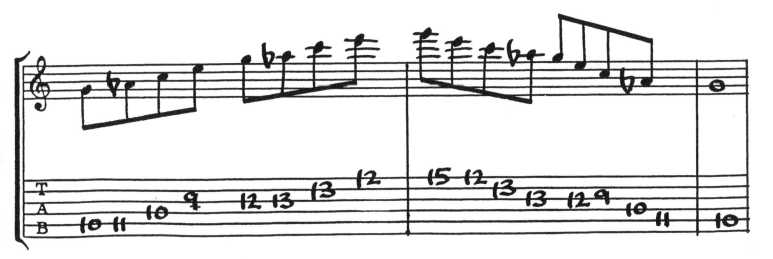

There are two more arpeggios that include E natural in them and if you're clever, you'd be noticing a pattern arising. That is, each time we extend the chord, it is the same as every alternate chord from the harmonized scale (a very strong reason to learn your harmonized scale) . So far we started with:

Dmin7b5 - Fmin (maj7) - Abmaj7#5

The next extension would be C7, according to the Harmonized scale, and then an Emin7b5. Both of these arpeggios include an E natural, which is specifically a D Aeolian b5 sound.

EXAMPLE 3 (c)   *C7 Arpeggio over Dmin7b5*

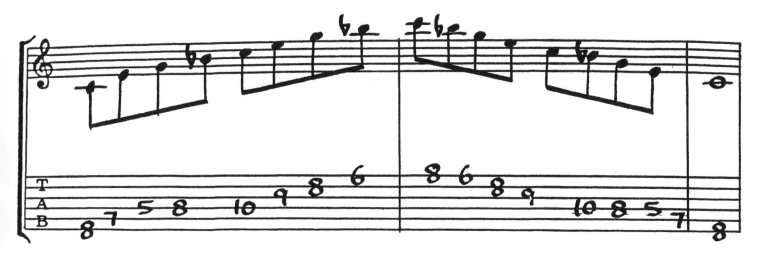

EXAMPLE 3 (d)   Emin7b5 Arpeggio over Dmin7b5

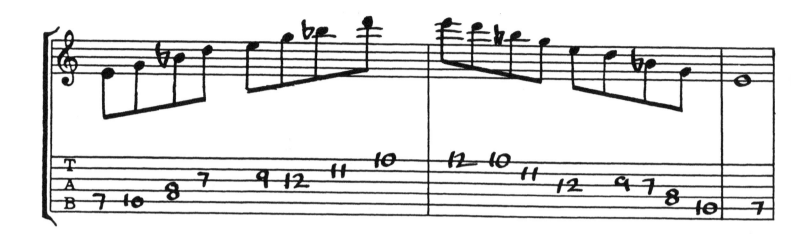

NOTE THERE IS POTENTIAL CONFUSION WITH THE FACT THAT THE 7TH CHORD OF THE MELODIC MINOR SCALE IS A MIN7b5 CHORD. THE OBVIOUS QUESTION ARISES, "WHY CAN'T WE PLAY MODE 7 OF THE MELODIC MINOR AS A POSSIBILITY FOR A MIN7b5 CHORD???" WELL, THE ANSWER TO THAT QUESTION IS THAT CHORD 7 IN MELODIC MINOR IS NOT REALLY FUNCTIONING AS A MIN7b5.. ALLOW ME TO EXPLAIN. LET'S TAKE "F" MELODIC MINOR.

F MELODIC MINOR = F G Ab Bb C D E

MODE 7 (SUPER LOCRIAN) = E F G Ab Bb C D = 1 b2 b3 3 b5 #5 b7

CHORD 7 OF F MELODIC MINOR = E MIN7b5

If we look closely at the interval structure of the Super Locrian you'll notice that we have two kinds of 3rd present, G = min 3rd of E. Ab = G# = natural 3rd of E.

Let's look at the structure of the Emin7b5 chord. Emin7b5 = E G Bb D = 1 b3 b5 b7. If this chord had the natural 3rd, (from the scale structure of the Super Locrian) we'd then have 1 3 b5 b7 = E G# Bb D = E7b5 = E dominant character.

Now let's take the minor 3rd we removed (G) and place it over the octave in the same chord. The G becomes the #9 of the chord. 1 3 b5 b7 #9 = E G# Bb D G = E7b5#9.

So you see, all we really did was add the natural 3rd to the min7b5 chord available to us in the 7th mode of melodic minor, and placed the minor 3rd over the octave, and we ended up with the true nature of the 7th degree of Melodic Minor. That is, a Dominant Altered sound and not a minor7b5 sound as disguised by the Harmonized Melodic Minor scale.

TRIADS IN D AEOLIAN b5 over D MIN7b5

There are two major triads in any melodic minor scale. They occur on the 4th and 5th degrees. F Melodic minor = D Aeolian b5. The 4th and 5th degrees of F are Bb and C. Therefore, the two major triads possible from D Aeolian b5 scale are Bb and C. The formula would be major triads on the b6 and b7 degrees of the minor7b5 chord.

EXAMPLE 4 (a)   *Bb MAJOR TRIAD over DMIN7b5*

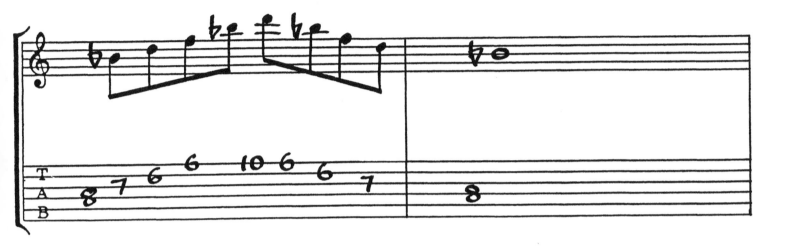

EXAMPLE 4 (b)   *C MAJOR TRIAD over DMIN7b5*

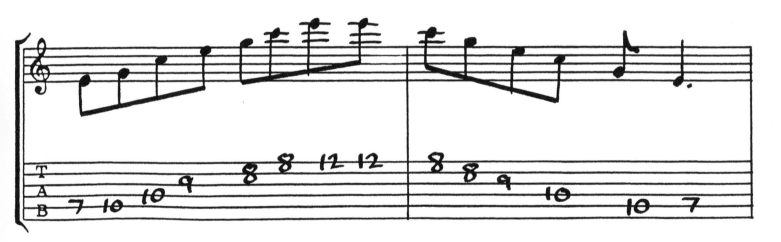

Don't forget that all the diatonic triads are possible ! ! !

EXAMPLE 4 (c)   *ALL D AEOLIAN b5 DIATONIC TRIADS over DMIN7b5*

INTERVALS FROM D AEOLIAN b5 over DMIN7b5

Let's listen to 3rds and 5ths.

EXAMPLE 5 (a)   *DIATONIC 3rds FROM D AEOLIAN b5 over DMIN7b5*

EXAMPLE 5 (b)   *DIATONIC 6ths FROM D AEOLIAN b5 over DMINb5*

SUMMARY OF MINOR7b5 AS VI CHORD MELODIC MINOR

Here now is a brief summary of recommended choices.

CHORD = D MIN7b5　　　　　　　　FORMULAS

SCALE = D AEOLIAN b5　　　　　　1 2 b3 4 b5 b6 b7
　　　　　　　　　　　　　　　　9 #9 11 #11 b13

PENTATONIC = HYBRID 2　　　　　1 2 b3 b5 b7

ARPEGGIOS = F MIN (MAJ7)　　　MIN (MAJ7) UP MIN 3RD,
　　　　　　　or Ab MAJ#5　　　MAJ7#5 UP A b5TH

TRIADS = C Major　　　　　　　Major triad from b7 of the
　　　　　　　　　　　　　　　chord root

INTERVAL = 3rds

D MIN7b5 AS CHORD II OF C HARMONIC MINOR

IF DMIN7b5 = C Harmonic Minor C D Eb G Ab B, then mode 2 = D Eb F G Ab B C. Let's compare these notes with D Major to discover the interval structure.

D Major = D E F# G A B C# = 1 2 3 4 5 6 7
(9) (11) (13)

Mode 2 C Harm. Min. = D Eb F G Ab B C = 1 b2 b3 4 b5 6 b7
(b9) (#9) (11) (#11) (13)

D Locrian Natural 6

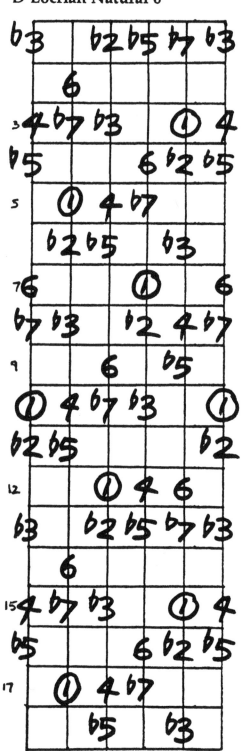

I will use the name LOCRIAN NATURAL 6 from this point for this mode. The note that makes this scale choice sound unique over a min7b5 is the natural 6.

HARMONIZED C HARMONIC MINOR:

Cmin(maj7) Dmin7b5 Ebmaj7#5 Fmin7 G7 Abmaj7 Bdim7

PENTATONICS IN D LOCRIAN NAT 6 OVER Dmin7b5

Once again there are no standard major or minor pentatonics within the Harmonic Minor scale, so it's time for some more interesting hybrids.

Scale structure = 1 b2 b3 4 b5 6 b7

If we incorporate the natural 6 in the hybrid pentatonics, we will discover sounds that are unique to the Locrian nat. 6.

EXAMPLE 1   *D LOCRIAN NAT. 6 OVER Dmin7b5*

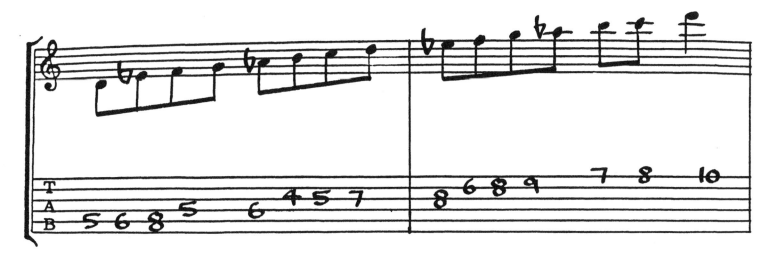

EXAMPLE 2 (a)   *HYBRID PENTATONIC 1. = 1 b3 4 b5 6*   *over Dmin7b5*

EXAMPLE 2 (b)   *HYBRID PENTATONIC 2. = 1 b3 b5 6 b7*   *over Dmin7b5*

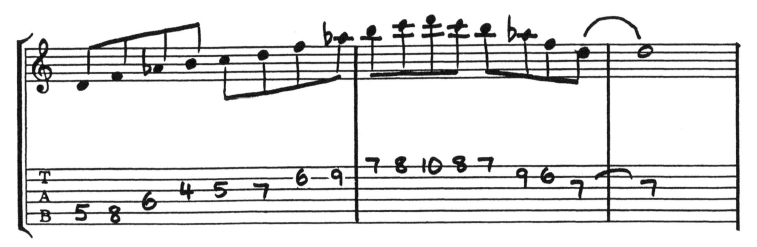

ARPEGGIOS FROM D LOCRIAN NAT6 OVER D MIN7b5

Chord I, III, and V in the harmonized harmonic minor scale are sounds we have already heard from the harmonized major scale. So, therefore, in the following section I'll only deal with the 4 remaining harmonized harmonic minor arpeggios.

Harmonized C Harmonic Minor scale =

Cmin (maj7)   Dmin7b5   Ebmaj7#5   Fmin7   G7   Abmaj7   Bdim7

We have obviously already listened to the Dmin7b5 arp. The Fmin7 arp was chord II of Eb Major (D Locrian), and Abmaj7 was chord IV of Eb Major scale (D Locrian).

So the remaining arps that we haven't heard yet, belonging to D LOCRIAN NAT6, are the following:

Cmin (maj7) - Ebmaj7#5 - G7 - Bdim7.

EXAMPLE 3 (a)   Cmin (maj7) ARPEGGIO OVER Dmin7b5

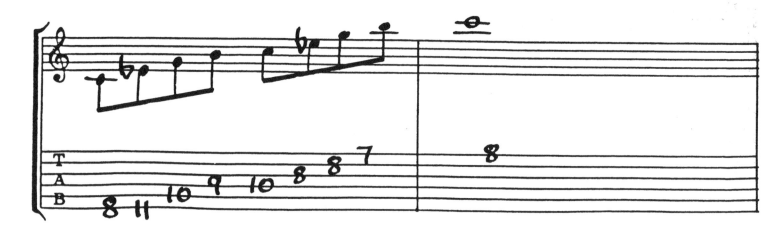

EXAMPLE 3 (b)   Ebmaj7#5 ARPEGGIO OVER Dmin7b5

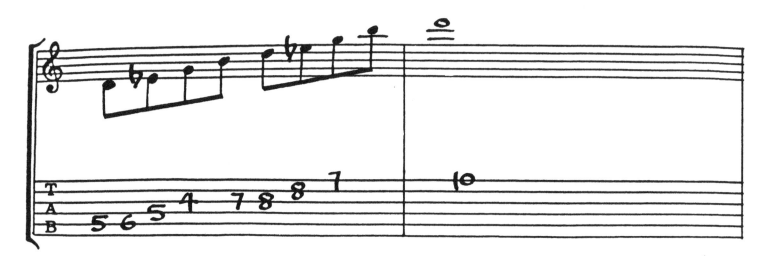

46

EXAMPLE 3 (c)   G7 ARPEGGIO OVER Dmin7b5

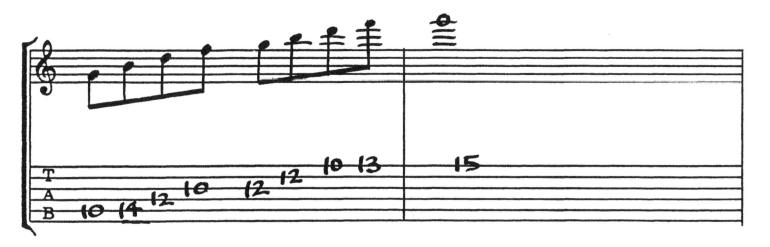

EXAMPLE 3 (d)   Bdim7 ARPEGGIO OVER Dmin7b5

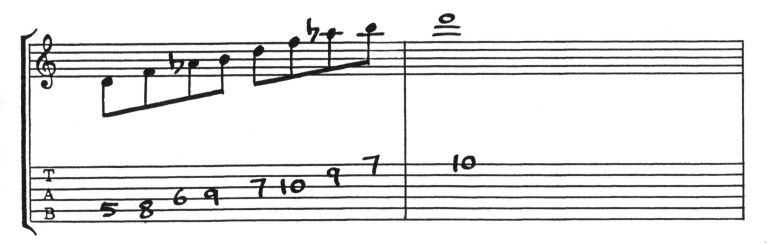

TRIADS FROM LOCRIAN NAT6 OVER Dmin7b5

There are 2 major triads in the Harmonic minor scale. They occur on the 5th and 6th degrees. So in C Harmonic minor, the 5th and 6th degrees are G and Ab. Therefore, the two triads are G and Ab Major. So from the D root of the Locrian nat 6, that means triads from the 4th and b5th degrees because the G and Ab are the 4th and b5th of D.

We have already heard one of the triads from the Locrian section; the Ab major triad which was the chord IV triad of Eb Major (D Locrian). So the triad that is uniquely a character of the D Locrian Nat6 scale approach is the "G" major.

EXAMPLE 4 (a)   G MAJOR TRIAD OVER Dmin7b5

Once again, don't forget that all the diatonic triads from the D Locrian nat 6 (C Harmonic Minor), are worth listening to.

EXAMPLE 4 (b)   ALL DIATONIC TRIADS FROM D LOCRIAN NAT6 OVER Dmin7b5

48

INTERVALS FROM D LOCRIAN NAT6 OVER Dmin7b5

We'll look at 3rds and 6ths.

EXAMPLE 5 (a)   *DIATONIC 3rds IN D LOCRIAN NAT6 OVER Dmin7b5*

EXAMPLE 5 (b)   *DIATONIC 6ths IN D LOCRIAN NAT6 OVER Dmin7b5*

SUMMARY OF MODE II HARMONIC MINOR OVER DMIN7b5

Here now are some of my recommendations from this chapter.

CHORD = Dmin7b5	FORMULAS
SCALE = D LOCRIAN NAT6	1 b2 b3 4 b5 6 b7 = D Eb F G Ab B C b9 #9 11 #11 13
PENTATONIC = HYBRID 2	1 b3 b5 6 b7 = D F Ab B C
ARPEGGIO = Cmin (maj7)	1 b3 5 7 C Eb G B Min (maj7) down a whole step from the root of the min7b5 chord
TRIAD = G Major	Major triad from the 4th of the min7b5 chord
INTERVALS	3rds or 6ths

TOTAL SUMMARY OF THE MINOR7b5

APPROACH	VII MAJ	VI MEL MIN	II HARM MIN
	7th mode - LOCRIAN	6th mode - AEOLIAN b5	2nd mode - LOCRIAN NAT6
SCALE	1 b2 b3 4 b5 b6 b7	1 2 b3 4 b5 b6 b7	1 b2 b3 4 b5 6 b7
PENTATONICS	up a 4th 1 b3 4 b6 b7	HYBRID 2 1 2 b3 b5 b7	HYBRID 2 1 b3 b5 6 b7
ARPEGGIO	maj7 up a b5th	maj7#5 up a b5th	down a whole step min (maj7) or up a 1/2 step maj7#5
TRIADS	major from the #5th degree	down a whole step major	major from the 4th degree
INTERVALS	4ths	3rds	6ths

NOTE All three of these scale approaches can be used at any time on a min7b5.

PROGRESSIONS TO PRACTICE USING MIN7b5 CHORDS

1. Use any of the three scale choices.

II:	Dmin7b5	I	%	I	%	I	%	I
I	Fmin7b5	I	%	I	%	I	%	I
I	Abmin7b5	I	%	I	%	I	%	I
I	Bmin7b5	I	%	I	%	I	%	:II

2. Any one of the 3 - Ab mel min - C dorian - Bb mel min. scales in ch. 5.

II:	Dmin7b5	I	%	I	G7#5b9	I	%	I
I	Cmin7	I	%	I	A7#5b9	I	%	:II.

3. "BEEF INTOLERABLE"
   (named after one of my favorite airline dishes).

A Aeolianb5 - Ab Lydian - G Mixolydian - F# Lydianb7-

F Dorian - B Super Locrian - Eb Major - D Mixolydian.

II:	Amin7b5	I	Abmaj7	I	F/G I	F#7b5	I
I	Fmin9	I	Bb7#59	I	Ebmaj7	I	C/D :II

51

"Beef Intolerable"

52

CHAPTER SIX:

DIMINISHED CHORDS

C Diminished

There are two ways of tackling the diminished chord. One way is with the obvious, the Diminished scale, and the second way is with the less obvious, mode VII of the Harmonic Minor.

First we'll discuss the Diminished scale. The Diminished scale from the roots C, Eb, Gb or A results in exactly the same notes. This is due to the min3rd symmetry of the diminished scale.

The chord we will use is Cdim7. The scale will be C Diminished.

C DIMINISHED scale compared to C Major:

C Major = C D E F G A B = 1 2 3 4 5 6 7 9 11 13

C Diminished = C D Eb F Gb Ab A B =
    1 2 b3 4 b5 b6 6 7 9 #9 11 #11 b13 13

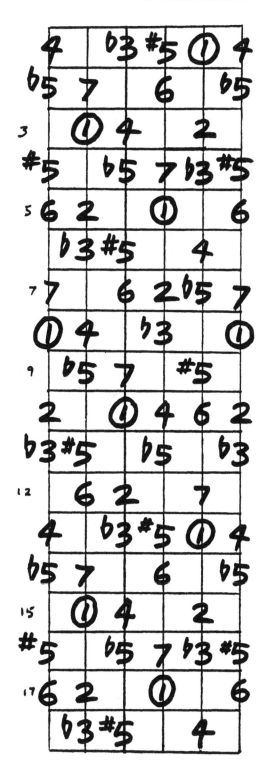

53

EXAMPLE 1   *C DIMINISHED SCALE OVER Cdim7*

PENTATONICS WITHIN THE DIMINISHED SCALE OVER C DIM7

Once again there are no standard major or minor pentatonics within the diminished scale, so let's look at our own hybrids.

Diminished scale structure = 1 2 b3 4 b5 #5 6 7 9 #9 11 #11 b13 13

From this information we find there are a number of 5 note pentatonic possibilities. The following examples feature all hybrid pentatonics over Cdim7.

EXAMPLE 2 (a)   *PENTATONIC HYBRID 1*   =   1 b3 4 b5 6   *over Cdim7*

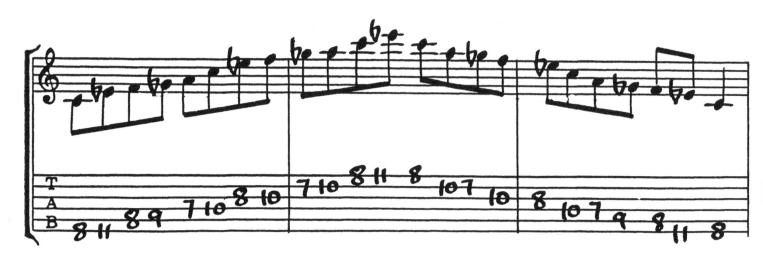

EXAMPLE 2 (b)   *PENTATONIC HYBRID 2*   =   *1 2 b3 b5 7*   *over Cdim7*

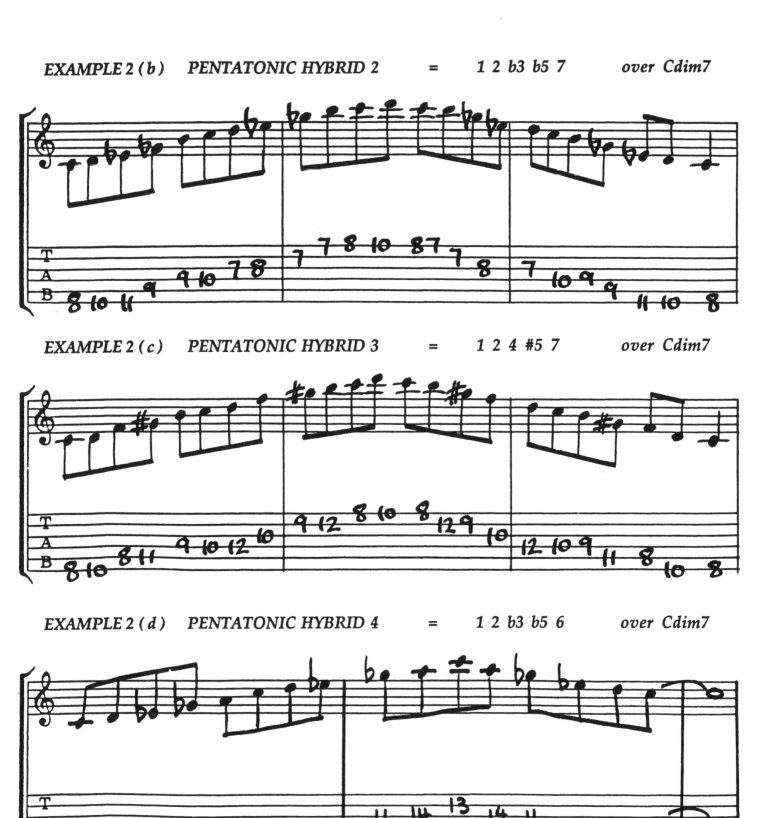

EXAMPLE 2 (c)   *PENTATONIC HYBRID 3*   =   *1 2 4 #5 7*   *over Cdim7*

EXAMPLE 2 (d)   *PENTATONIC HYBRID 4*   =   *1 2 b3 b5 6*   *over Cdim7*

Feel free to experiment with other possibilities taken from the diminished scale's interval structure.

ARPEGGIOS FROM C DIMINISHED SCALE OVER C DIM7

Let's take a closer look at the chords available to us from the diminished scale.

The diminished scale is constructed from the notes of two diminished 7th chords a whole step apart. Let me show you. Usually when we construct a harmonized scale we take every other note from the scale, e. g. :

C DIM scale = 1 2 b3 4 b5 6 7 = C D Eb F Gb Ab A B

C Eb Gb and A = Cdim7 chord, alternately,

D F Ab and B = Ddim7 chord.

So you see that combining the notes of two diminished 7 chords a whole step apart gives us a diminished scale. This information is useful for creating unusual sounds over a diminished chord and helps make the diminished scale somewhat more ambiguous, because now you know that certain patterns will work up a whole step, instead of always moving in the predictable min 3rd fashion so closely associated with this symmetrical scale.

So basically you can play a dim7 arpeggio from every step of this scale. This will be example 3 (d).

Let's look at other arpeggios available from the scale:

1 2 b3 4 b5 #5 6 7 = C D Eb F Gb Ab A B

By looking at the scale, it is easy seeing the chord possibilities.

1 b3 b5 6 = C Eb Gb and A = Cdim7

1 b3 b5 7 = C Eb Gb and B = Cmin (maj7) b5. That's a particularly ugly name for this chord and luckily for all of us, there's a simpler name.

Eb = D#, Gb = F#. "So ?", you ask. Well now we see that we have a C with D# F# and B. The notes D# F# and B = B maj triad. So, a simpler name for this Cmin (maj7) #5 would be Bmaj over a C root. "B/C"

1 b3 #5 7 = C Eb G# B = Cmin(maj7)#5. There's an easier name for this: G# = Ab; B = Cb; Ab, Cb & Eb = Abmin. So Cmin(maj7)#5 = Abmin/C.

So the lesson here is that if you know the notes in a chord and you know the root, sometimes just rearranging the remaining notes gives you a 3 or 4 note chord that is familiar. Then all you do is name that chord (sounds like a T. V. show), then place it over the slash of the root note.

EXAMPLE 3 (a)   C DIM7 ARPEGGIO OVER C DIM7 CHORD

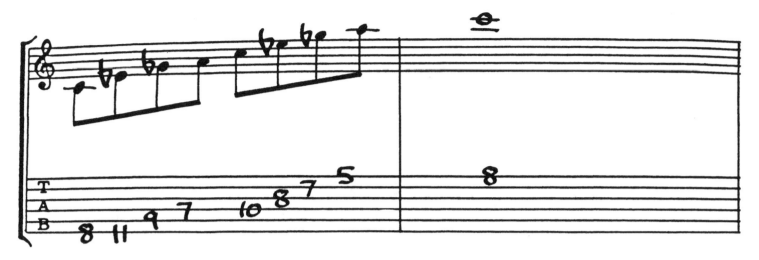

EXAMPLE 3 (b)   B/C ARPEGGIO OVER C DIM7 CHORD

EXAMPLE 3 (c)   Abmin/C ARPEGGIO OVER C DIM7 CHORD

EXAMPLE 3 (*d*) DIM 7 ARPS FROM ALL DIM SCALE TONES OVER C DIM7 CHORD

TRIADS FROM THE C DIMINISHED SCALE OVER C DIM7 CHORD

Major triads in the Diminished scale occur in minor 3rd intervals beginning down a 1/2 step from the root of the scale. Therefore, in C Diminished we have B D F and Ab major triads. Another way to visualize them would be to think of them from the 2nd - 4th - #5th - maj7th degrees from the root of the diminished chord.

EXAMPLE 4 (*a*) D MAJOR TRIAD OVER C DIM7

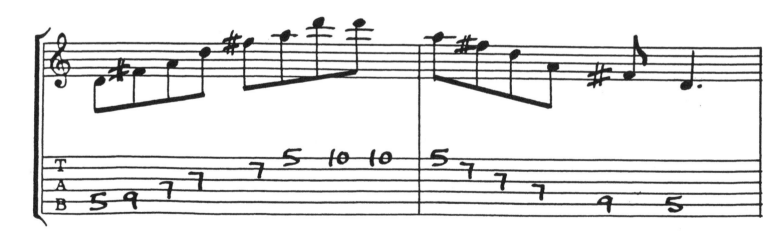

EXAMPLE 4 (b)   *F MAJOR TRIAD OVER C DIM7*

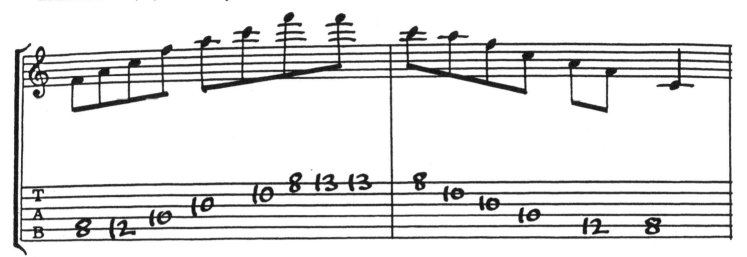

EXAMPLE 4 (c)   *Ab MAJOR TRIAD OVER C DIM7*

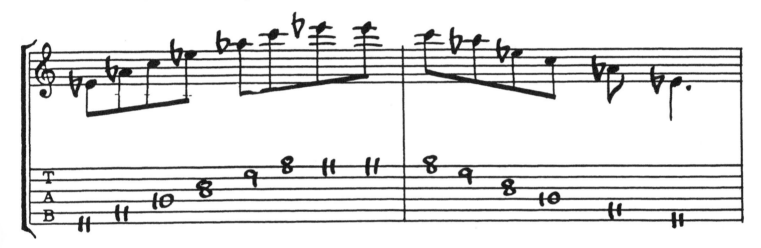

EXAMPLE 4 (d)   *B MAJOR TRIAD OVER C DIM7*

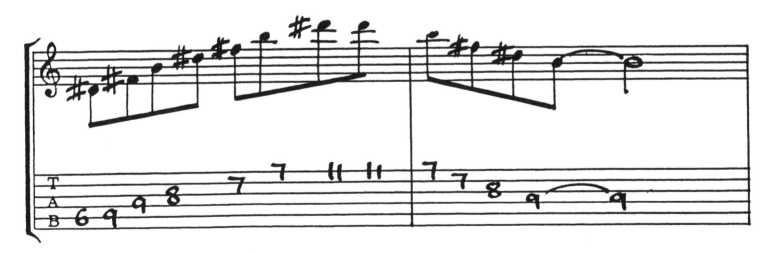

NOTE All these major triads could also be minor, so try those too!

INTERVALS WITHIN THE DIMINISHED SCALE OVER C DIM7

Minor 3rds and 6ths move symmetrically up and down the scale steps.

EXAMPLE 5 (a)   PARALLEL MIN 3rds OVER C DIM7 CHORD

EXAMPLE 5 (b)   PARALLEL 6ths OVER C DIM7 CHORD

Major 3rd intervals move in min 3rd increments beginning down a 1/2 step from the root of the chord.

EXAMPLE 5 (c)   *MAJ 3rds IN MIN 3rd INCREMENTS OVER C DIM7 CHORD*

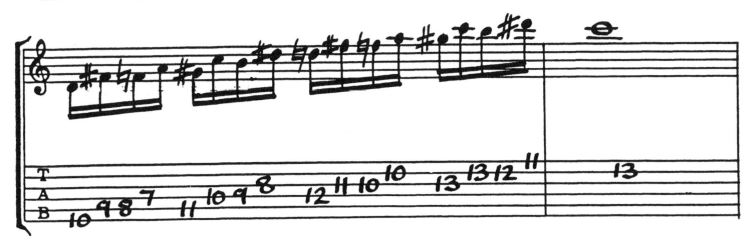

4ths also move symmetrically in min3rd increments beginning from the root of the diminished chord.

EXAMPLE 5 (d)   *4ths IN MIN3rd INCREMENTS OVER C DIM7 CHORD*

SUMMARY OF C DIMINISHED SCALE OVER C DIM7 CHORD

CHORD = C DIM7	FORMULAS
SCALE = C DIMINISHED SCALE	1 2 b3 4 b5 #5 6 7 (9) (11) (b13) (13)
PENTATONIC = HYBRID 4	1 2 b3 b5 6
ARPEGGIOS = B/C	1 b3 b5 7
TRIADS = D, F, Ab, B	Triads from the 2nd, 4th, b5th & 6th degrees from the root of the dim7 chord.
INTERVALS = min 3rds or 4ths	

61

DIM7 AS CHORD VII OF HARMONIC MINOR

Mode VII F Harmonic Minor

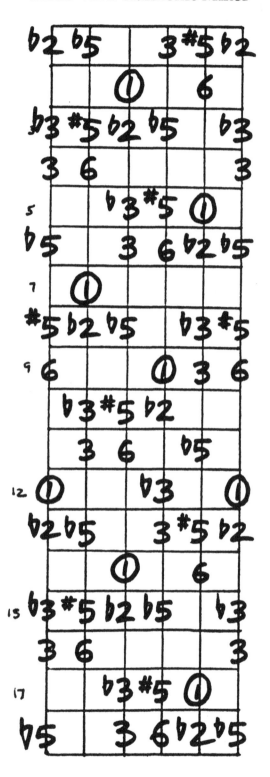

The 7th chord of the Harmonic minor scale is a diminished 7th chord. This means that the 7th mode of the Harmonic minor can be played over a diminished chord. Let's analyze it. Edim7 will be our example chord. So, Edim7 is the the 7th chord of F Harmonic minor.

F Harmonic minor = F G Ab Bb C Db E

Mode VII = E F G Ab (G#) Bb C Db =
       1 b2 b3 3 b5 #5 6 b9 #9 #11 b13 13

EXAMPLE 1 MODE VII F HARMONIC MINOR OVER Edim7

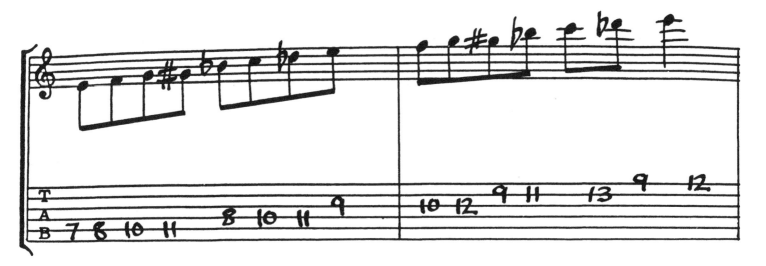

NOTE Because of the unusual nature of the interval structure of this mode, no name is really possible other than mode VII harmonic minor. So that is what we will call it throughout this section.

PENTATONICS FROM MODE VII F HARM MIN OVER E DIM7 CHORD

As you've probably guessed, there are no standard major or minor pentatonics within the Harmonic minor scale. It's time for hybrids again.

Intervallic structure = 1 b2 b3 3 b5 #5 6

EXAMPLE 2 (a)   PENTATONIC HYBRID 1 = 1 b3 b5 #5 6 OVER E DIM7

EXAMPLE 2 (b)   PENTATONIC HYBRID 2 = 1 b2 3 b5 6 OVER E DIM7

EXAMPLE 2 (c)   PENTATONIC HYBRID 3 = 1 b2 b3 b5 6 OVER DIM7

ARPEGGIOS FROM MODE VII HARMONIC MINOR OVER DIM7 CHORD

There are 7 arpeggios to investigate from the harmonized harmonic minor scale. They are as follows:

Fmin (maj7) Gmin7b5 Abmaj7#5 Bbmin7 C7 Dbmaj7 Edim7

Let's have a listen to all of these.

EXAMPLE 3 (a)   *Fmin (MAJ7) ARPEGGIO OVER E DIM7*

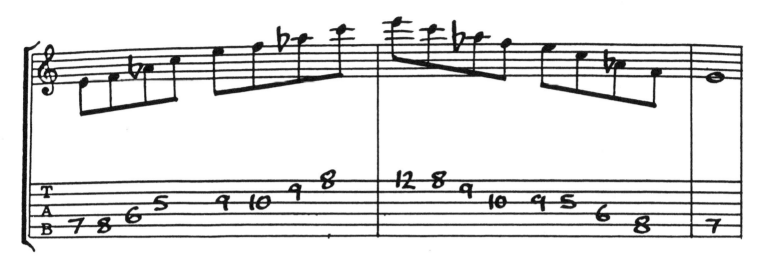

EXAMPLE 3 (b)   *Gmin7b5 ARPEGGIO OVER E DIM7*

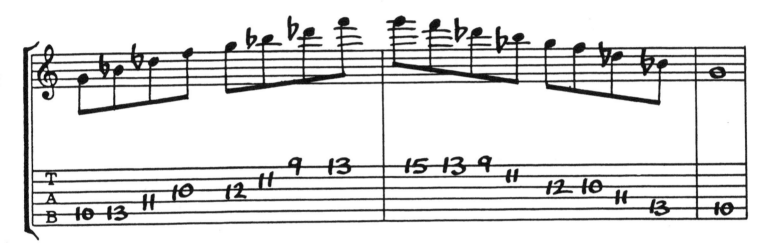

EXAMPLE 3 (c)   *Abmaj7#5 ARPEGGIO OVER DIM7*

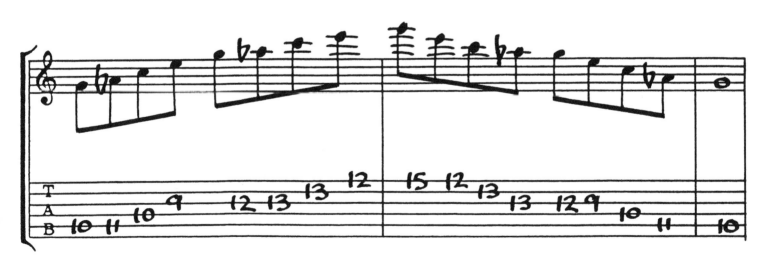

EXAMPLE 3 (d)   Bbmin7 ARPEGGIO OVER E DIM7

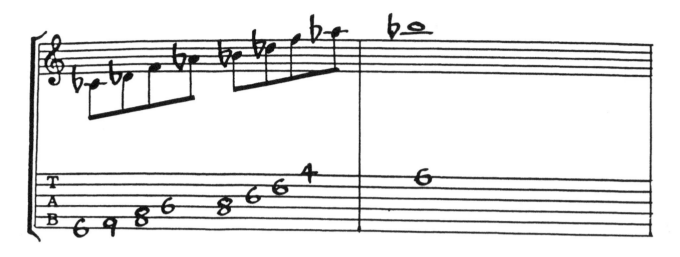

EXAMPLE 3 (e)   C7 ARPEGGIO OVER E DIM7

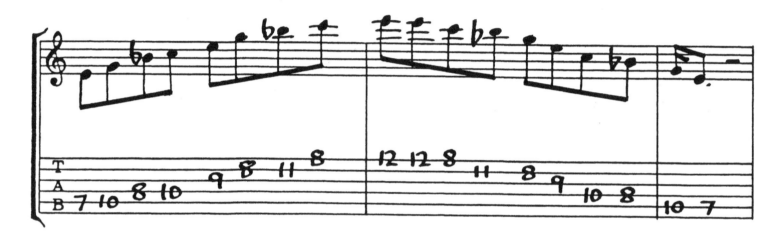

EXAMPLE 3 (f)   Dbmaj7 ARPEGGIO OVER E DIM7

EXAMPLE 3 (g)   Edim7 ARPEGGIO OVER E DIM7

TRIADS FROM MODE VII HARMONIC MINOR OVER DIM7

There are two major triads in the Harmonic minor scale. They appear on the 5th and 6th degrees of the scale. Therefore, the 5th and 6th degrees of F Harmonic minor would be C and Db. This is the same as the #5th and 6th degrees from the root of the Edim7 chord because C and Db are the #5 and natural 6 of E. Let's listen to these two triads.

EXAMPLE 4 (a)   C MAJOR TRIAD OVER E DIM7

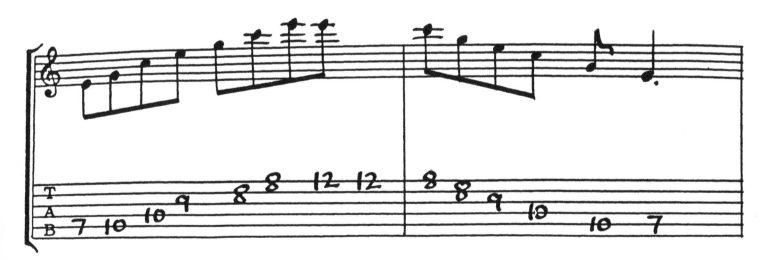

EXAMPLE 4 (b)   Db MAJOR TRIAD OVER E DIM7

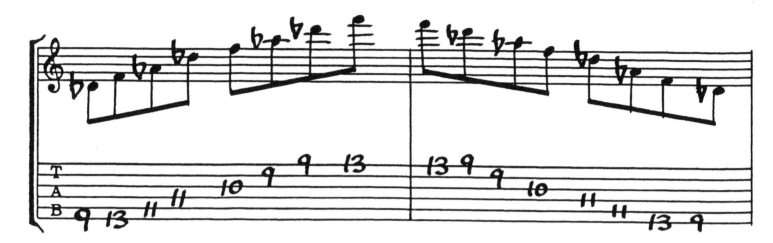

Let's take a look at the harmonized scale for the harmonic minor again to discover the remaining triads.

Scale chords for F Harmonic minor in triads.

Fmin - Gdim - Abaug - Bbmin - C - Db - Edim

We've already heard the C and Db triads. Edim and Gdim we've also heard; they both consist of chord tones from Edim7. So let's hear the ones remaining that sound specifically like VII mode Harmonic minor.

EXAMPLE 4 (c&d) Fmin and Ab aug TRIADS OVER E DIM7

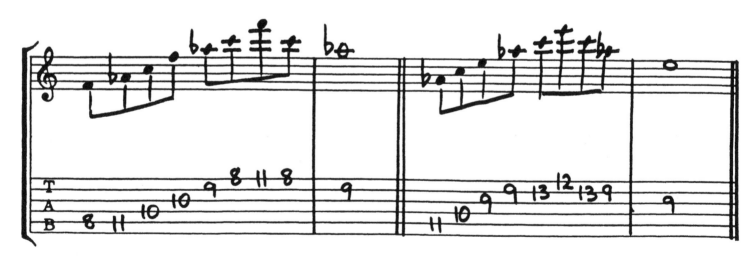

EXAMPLE 4 (e)   *Bbmin TRIAD OVER E DIM7*

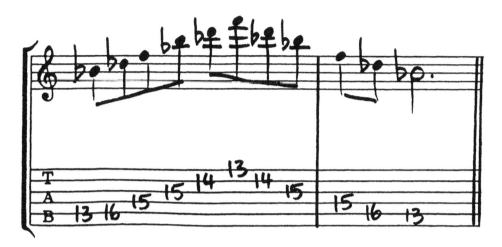

INTERVALS WITHIN MODE VII HARMONIC MINOR OVER E DIM7

3rds and 6ths sound good. Let's listen to those.

EXAMPLE 5 (a)   *DIATONIC 3rds FROM MODE VII HARM MIN OVER E DIM7*

EXAMPLE 5 (b)   *DIATONIC 6ths FROM MODE VII HARM MIN OVER E DIM7*

SUMMARY OF MODE VII HARMONIC MINOR OVER DIM7

Here now are some recommendations.

CHORD = E DIM7	FORMULAS
SCALE = MODE VII HARMONIC MINOR	1 b2 b3 3 b5 #5 6 (b9) (#9) (#11) (b13) (13) [E F G G# Bb C C#]
PENTATONICS = HYBRID 3	1 b2 b3 b5 6 = E F G Bb C#
ARPEGGIO = Gmin7b5	min7b5 up a min3rd
TRIADS = C or Db major	major triads on the #5 or 6th degree of the chord
INTERVAL	Min 3rds

PROGRESSIONS TO PRACTICE USING DIM7 CHORDS

1.   D Aeolian - Mode VII Harm Min - C Mel Min - G Mixolydian

II:	Dmin	I	%	I	C#dim7	I	%	I
I	Cmin6	I	%	I	G/B	I	%	:II

2.   "CLEO & REBECCA"

G Major - G#Dim - A Dorian - D Mixolydian - Eb Dim - E Aeolian - G Mixolydian - C# Dim - D Mixolydian

II:	G	I	%	I	G#dim7	I	%	I
I	Amin7	I	%	I	C/D	I	Ebdim7	I
I	Emin7	I	%	I	F/G	I	%	I
I	C#dim7	I	%	I	C/D	I	%	:II

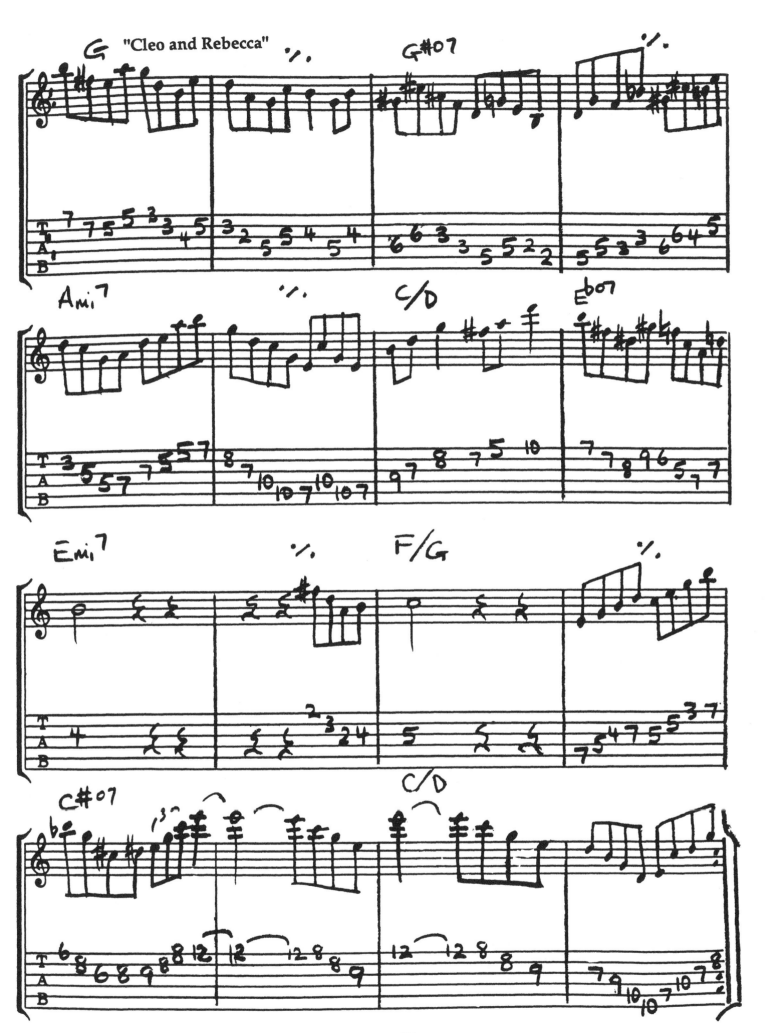

"Cleo and Rebecca"

Well, that's about it for the theory lesson so far folks. I hope this info strikes a few unsolved musical problem monsters clean on the head. I also hope you find yourself picking some new licks. Then I will have succeeded in stretching your brain and expanding the old grey matter.

Good Luck Guitar Players!